It's Alive*

Math like you've never known it before ...
and like you may never know it again

by Asa Kleiman and David Washington
with Mary Ford Washington

Illustrated by Eric Nelson

*Void where prohibited by law

ISBN 1-882664-27-2

PRUFROCK PRESS INC

PRUFROCK PRESS
P.O. Box 8813
Waco, TX 76714-8813
Phone: (800) 998-2208
Fax: (800) 240-0333
www.prufrock.com

Contents

Note to teachers:

If someone in your class asks, "May we use calculators?"
Our answer is, "Are mice rodents? Is Asa's sister annoying? Will Jane marry Bob?"
Yes, you can use calculators.

The bold facts in this book are true.
(Everything else is horsefeathers.)

Sources

Andrews, Michael (1977). *The Life that Lives on Man*. Taplinger Publishing: New York.

Conniff, Richard (July 1995). When It Comes to the Pesky Flea, Ignorance is Bliss. *Smithsonian Magazine*, 77-78.

Elfman, Eric (1994). *Almanac of the Gross, Disgusting & Totally Repulsive*. Random House: New York.

Information Please Environmental Almanac (1994). Houghton Mifflin: Boston.

Information Please Almanac, Atlas and Yearbook (1992). Houghton Mifflin: Boston.

Marshfield Wastewater Treatment Center, Marshfield, WI.

Nash, Bartleby (1991). *Mother Nature's Greatest Hits: The Top 40 Wonders of the Animal World*. Living Planet Press: Los Angeles.

National Center for Health Statistics, 1992.

New Grolier's Multimedia Encyclopedia. Grolier Electronic Publishing: Danbury, CT.

Smithsonian Magazine, April 1995.

Thomas, Lewis (1974). *The Lives of a Cell*. Bantam Books: Toronto.

Thomas, Warren, and Kaufman, Daniel (1990). *Dolphin Conferences, Elephant Midwives, and Other Astonishing Facts About Animals*. Tarcher: Los Angeles.

US Department of Agriculture, 1991.

World Health Organization, United Nations, 1990.

Using Really Big Numbers

Big numbers are easy when you remember three things:

☞ each group of three numbers is called a period;

☞ each period has a ones place, tens place, and hundreds place;

☞ reading from left to right, you say the name of the group at the comma.

Number of commas	Name
1	thousand
2	million
3	billion
4	trillion
5	quadrillion
6	quintillion
7	sextillion
8	septillion
9	octillion
10	nonillion
11	decillion
12	undecillion
13	duodecillion
14	tredecillion
15	quattuordecillion
16	quindecillion
17	sexdecillion
18	septendecillion
19	octodecillion
20	novemdecillion
21	vigintillion
33	googol

So...

1,345,768,095,438 is read
1 trillion, 345 billion, 768 million, 95 thousand, 438

No big deal, right?

About ¾ of known animal species are arthropods — animals
like flies, spiders, scorpions, moths, crayfish, centipedes, etc.

If everyone at your school is dressing up as a different animal for the
upcoming Halloween party, and there are 600 people in the school,
how many should come dressed as arthropods?

Keep with the 3/4 of known animals are arthropods.

1

Arctic terns fly round trip from the Arctic to the Antarctic
each year. That's 11,000 miles one way.

If Arctic terns could collect one frequent flier mile for every mile they
fly, how many frequent flier miles could an Arctic tern collect over a
20-year period?

2

About 10 billion skin scales peel off each of our bodies every day.

How many skin scales can you expect to peel off your body in the next 20 minutes?

(Kindly refrain from shedding on the book.)

3

Asa and David poured a 48-ounce container of school lunch gravy through a strainer. After straining, the gravy weighed in at 26 ounces.

What percent of the gravy would not go through the strainer?

4

Yankee Stadium seats 57,600 spectators.

At the last baseball game, David and Asa's independent research found gum stuck to the bottom of 2 out of 3 seats, in a variety of flavors and colors.

If their research is correct, exactly how many seats in Yankee Stadium actually have gum stuck to them and what flavors are they?

Prolonged exposure to 85 decibels can lead to deafness.

If your school bell rings at 118 decibels, and someone lucky enough to get caught under it when it rings jumps 4½ centimeters per decibel, how high do they jump?

If David's yard measures 110' x 25' and is tightly packed with snow 2 feet deep, how many cubic-foot bricks of snow are available for him to build a scale model of the Taj Mahal?

7

Asa's big toe is shorter than his middle toe. David's big toe is longer than his other toes.

Which one of your toes is the longest? Graph toe length for students in your class.

big toe	second toe	middle toe	second-to-last toe	pinky toe

8

David and Asa have calculated the percent of houses in their town with each type of lawn ornament listed below:

- 👉 18 percent—Snow White and the seven dwarfs
- 👉 7 percent—crystal balls (no doubt useful for fortune telling)
- 👉 6 percent—little Mexican boys leading little Mexican donkeys
- 👉 14 percent—cutesy squirrels and bunnies
- 👉 17 percent—Bambi and his relatives (outfitted in orange during hunting season)
- 👉 25 percent—black boys fishing
- 👉 3 percent—white boys fishing

If there are 20,000 people in their town and approximately 5 people live in each house, how many houses have each kind of lawn ornament?

9

300,000 species of beetles have been identified by scientists, but scientists believe there are really a lot more — probably as many as 12 million species of beetles.

If this is true, what fraction have been identified by science so far?

What percent? (And what's that swimming in your soup?)

10

The school janitor has been keeping a record of things she finds on the floor when she sweeps up after school.

On Tuesday of this week she found:

2,184 chawed off pencils

18 purple wads of gum

26 chawed off pens

12 detention slips (unsigned)

2 dimes

1 arthropod

14 erasers

1 Barney watch

117 wadded up homework assignments

1 master list of passwords for the central school computer

17 pink wads of gum

11 fuzzy green wads of gum

14 permission slips (unsigned)

1 ransom note (signed)

3 empty juice boxes

142 squashed raisins

1 copy of this book

1 partridge in a pear tree

☞ How many things did she find on the floor?

☞ How many more chawed off pencils did she find than wads of gum?

☞ What is the ratio of detention slips to permission slips?

☞ What percent of the total garbage was the arthropod?

11

Someone who didn't have anything better to do determined that Americans eat an average of 32,850 acres of pizza a year.

How much is this a day?

12

The average person in America will live to the age of 72, and consume 40 tons of food in his or her lifetime.

If Asa has eaten and continues to eat nothing but ¼-pound cans of Spam™ for his entire life, how many total cans of Spam™ will Asa eat in his lifetime?

13

The average pair of socks traps about 190 milligrams of skin a day.

If Asa wears his socks two (non-leap) years straight without changing them, how much heavier will they be when he finally takes them off?

14

How far did a fly which nibbled its way around the edge of David's mom's 9" x 13" prune frosted tofu cake walk?

15

As many as 5 million mites have been found crowded together in one square inch.

How many mites could be sitting on this 8½" x 11" page staring at you right this minute?

16

Two-thirds of skin scales examined in the laboratory are found to be contaminated with large colonies of bacteria.

If your school lunch cook absent-mindedly scratches 800 skin scales off into the lukewarm chicken noodle soup, how many large colonies of bacteria just dropped into the soup?

Of course, this does not happen in your school.

(Hopefully.)

17

At Asa's house there is a candy jar in the living room which is ⅓ full of good fruit candies and ⅔ full of deadly butterscotch candies.

How many deadly butterscotch candies should Asa expect to find in any handful which contains 12 candies?

18

Frogs lay 3,000 eggs at a time.

You have found yourself floating in a pond surrounded by eggs from 147 pairs of daddy and mommy frogs. How many frogs will be surrounding you when the eggs have all hatched?

19

Your science book may not have told you this, but Demodex mites, which look like 8-legged crocodiles through a microscope, live on everyone's eyelashes.

Although harmless, these teeny tiny mites slither down eyelashes into the eyelid in order to lay their heart-shaped eggs. It takes one of these mites about 4 minutes to travel 20 mm down an eyelash.

How long will it take one of these mites to slither the full length of an eyelash which is 1 cm long?

20

While playing a computer game, David was eating grapes out of a bag. The bag contained 62 grapes when it was full, and it is now ⅔ empty. David has not noticed, but 14 percent of the grapes in the bag are old and fuzzy.

How many old, fuzzy grapes has David eaten?

21

David figures he has about 320 ideas a day, but at least 75 percent of these ideas get interrupted — either by his sister, his other sister, his other sister, his mom, the telephone, etc. Of the interrupted ideas, ⅓ return later.

According to these estimates, how many ideas does David lose every day?

22

There are 2,451 air miles between New York and Los Angeles. There are 62,000 miles of blood vessels in your body.

If you stood in New York and stretched your blood vessels all the way to Los Angeles and then back again to New York and then to Los Angeles and so on, would you finish closer to New York or to Los Angeles?

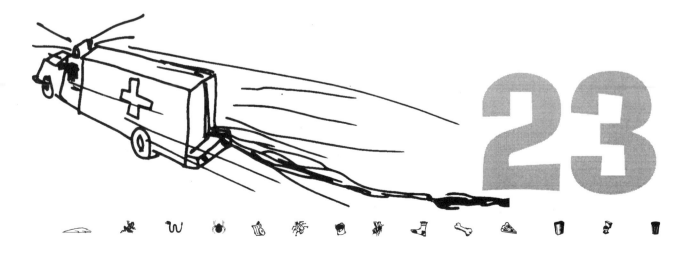

23

The human brain will store 100 trillion bits in its lifetime.

8 bits equal 1 byte, and 1,024 bytes equal 1 kilobyte, and 1,024 kilobytes equal one megabyte.

How many million megabytes can your brain store?

24

If a 1,000-megabyte hard drive costs you about $300, how much would a hard drive equivalent to your brain cost (assuming price is based on megabytes)?

25

The human brain runs at about 25 megahertz.

A computer runs at about 120 megahertz.

Make up your own problem. (The computer is already done.)

26

Skin houses an average of 32 million bacteria per square inch. Because bacteria thrive on moisture, under waterproof bandages they can increase their populations up to 10,000 times.

After David's last bike crash he carefully put a 1" waterproof bandage over his mangled elbow. How many bacteria could be clinging to David's elbow when he finally gets the courage to peel the bandage off?

27

It has been reported that 17 out of a thousand people have frequent indigestion.

Asa and David have done their own (questionable) research, studying the effects of eating habits on indigestion. They found that in any group of 5,000 people:

☞ 364 of them eat cold pizza and cola (that's all they eat, cold pizza and cola)

☞ 325 of them can consume a foot-long sub in less than 65 seconds

(Of the above, 25 percent can consume a sub in less than 10 seconds)

☞ 274 of them consider monosodium glutamate an essential nutrient

☞ 472 of them will eat anything just so that it won't go to waste

☞ 625 of them will eat anything they have a coupon for

☞ 170 of them eat peas porridge in the pot (nine days old)

☞ 69 of them have the motto, "Everything is better with gravy."

☞ 12 of them eat peanut butter and jellyfish sandwiches

According to the statistic, how many of each of the groups listed above might have frequent indigestion?

A bat eats about 3,000 mosquitoes in one night.

Last time Asa and David went camping, they counted about 27,000 mosquitoes in their tent (give or take a few). How many bats should they bring along next time?

29

There are 6 boxes of cereal in David's household. The wheat bran flakes will last 4 months (David's mom is the only one who eats these), the Frosted Mini-Wheats™ will last 3½ weeks, the Rice Krispies™ will last 4 weeks, the Cheerios™ will last a week and a half, the Apple Squares™ only last 1 week, and the All Bran™ will never be eaten by anybody.

If all the boxes are presently full, how many boxes of cereal will David's mom have to buy in the next 12 months?

30

Every morning beginning on March 28th, Asa pours a small bowlful of Lucky Charms™, scoops out all of the little yellow moon marshmallows from the bowl, and puts them in a clear plastic bag in his closet.

How many little yellow moon marshmallows does Asa have in his closet by the end of September, if the cereal averages 17 little yellow moon marshmallows per bowl?

(Asa insists we include this problem.)

31

Asa's dog, Spot, fertilized the back yard in 400 evenly distributed places. The yard is 100' long x 100' wide.

If, as you are walking, you cover 10 square feet of Asa's yard, what is the probability that you will need to scrape Spot's droppings off the sole of your shoe?

32

At the local grocery store bulletin board, Asa and David found these 10 signs. Create three problems of your own based on these signs.

Are you Illiterate? If so, call 1-800-CANT-READ.

Time Travelers' Meeting: 7:45 p.m. last Tuesday.

PSYCHICS' MEETING: You Know Where. You Know When.

Weight Watchers: $14 All You Can Eat
Hot Fudge Sundae and Cheesecake Dinner.

Central Wisconsan Computer Club: "Learning to Use Spell Check"
Meat in the Lobby of Super 8 Motel, 8-9 p.m., Wednesday.

Antique Collectors Display:
Pentium Computers, Then and Now.
See our collection dating all the way back to 1995.

TIME MANAGEMENT WORKSHOP for people who find themselves
just too busy. Meetings 6:30-9:30 weekly, attendance mandatory.

Janitors Wanted, $42,000 starting salary. Ph.D. required.

Seven-eighths of David's math class have their watches synchronized to beep irritatingly five minutes before the end of math class.

If there are 32 people in David's math class, how many students will his teacher detain after class?

34

There are about 100 billion bacteria presently living on your body, most of which are very helpful. The average life of a bacteria is only 20 minutes.

How long until all the bacteria presently living on your body go on to bacteria heaven?

35

Leeches drink up to eight times their weight in one sitting.

If you were a 90-pound pop-drinking leech, how many 12-ounce cans of soda pop could you drink in one sitting?

36

Bacteria love moisture and warmth. For this reason, taking a bath can actually triple the number of bacteria on your skin. If the bacteria found per square centimeter on an average person before a bath are as follows:

50,000 on your back

200,000 on your forehead

1,000,000 in your armpit

1,500,000 on your scalp

How many bacteria would there be in each spot after bathing?

37

Adult salt-water crocodiles enjoy eating people. It has been reported that as many as 2,000 people around the world are eaten by salt-water crocodiles each year.

If there are 5.9 billion people in the world, what are your chances of being eaten by a crocodile in the coming year?

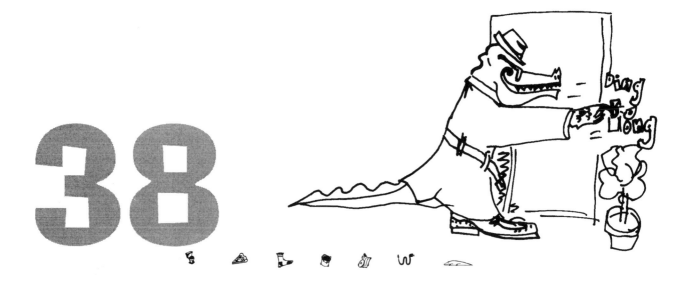

38

Cows pass a lot of gas. In fact, American cattle add as much as 300,000 tons of methane gas to the atmosphere each day.

If all this cow gas could be collected and sold at gas stations for fuel (let's say gas stations charged $1.25 a pound for cow gas) how much would the country's total cow gas output per day be worth?

39

One spray of skunk scent can be smelled for more than a mile in any direction.

How many square miles can a skunk stink in one spray?

(Try saying that 10 times fast.)

40

Air from a big sneeze can travel 104 miles an hour.

Asa is about to sneeze, and it's going to be a big one. How far away should David stand if the sneeze particles will be airborne for 2½ seconds? (There are 5,280 feet in a mile.)

41

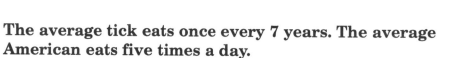

The average human has 9,000 taste buds.

David's sister ate an entire bag of incredibly sour candies and burned off 47 percent of her taste buds in the process. How many taste buds does she have left?

42

The average tick eats once every 7 years. The average American eats five times a day.

How many times more often do Americans eat?

43

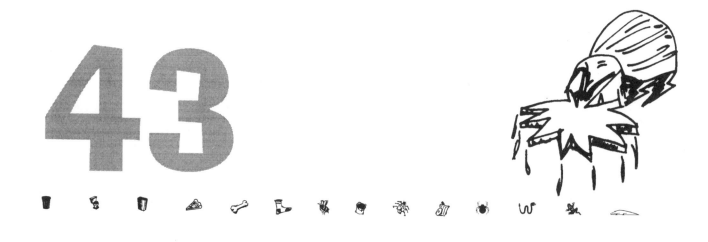

The average toilet uses 1½ gallons of water per flush.

If a city's wastewater treatment plant has three 100,000-gallon capacity tanks for processing toilet water, how many toilets flushing at once would it take to overflow the city's tank?

44

There are 5½ billion humans in the world. There are 40 septillion nematode sea worms in the world.

Divided equally, how many nematode sea worms could each person in the world adopt as pets?

45

Each year 1,000 cats in the United States have heart operations to receive pacemakers, at a cost of $800 each.

What would you do with $800,000?

46

The heart pumps 2,000 gallons of blood each day.

Lake Michigan contains 1.3 quadrillion gallons of water.

How long would it take your heart to pump Lake Michigan dry?

(Warning: Do not try this experiment at home.)

47

One acre of good soil usually contains about three million worms.

How many worms can Asa and David expect to find between each 10-yard line as they dig up the perfectly manicured grass on the junior high school football field?

(1 acre = 4,840 square yards)

48

Taxpayers spent $23.4 million on the toilet system for the US space shuttle.

Assuming the toilet has been used 1,209 times (we were unable to locate any actual statistics on this), and assuming the astronauts always remembered to flush, how much has the space shuttle toilet cost per flush?

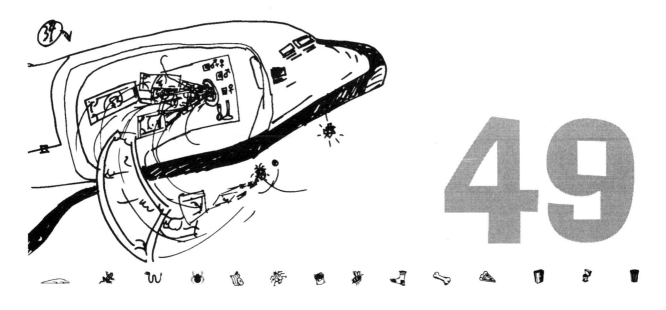

49

The diameter of a basketball is about 9".

The diameter of a giant squid eyeball is 15".

If you were playing basketball with a giant squid eyeball and totally deflated it (through no fault of your own), how many cubic inches of giant squid eyeball juice would seep out onto the floor?

(The formula to find the volume of a sphere is ⅘ x π x r³.)

50

It is estimated that there are 25 million assorted insects hanging in the air over every square mile of U.S. land (excluding Alaska and Hawaii).

During his first week attending Camp Torture (10 square miles of Wisconsin swampland) Asa was bitten by 1,738 insects. Asa's counselor comforted him by saying, "Look kid, just think how many insects didn't bite you." How many Camp Torture insects did not bite Asa?

51

David figures that his older sister spends 14 percent of her waking life every day in front of the mirror. If she sleeps 8 hours each day, how much time each day does she spend in front of the mirror?

52

Answer Key

Warning: answers may vary due to rounding. That's cool.

1

Halloween arthropods

¾ of the 600 people should come dressed as arthropods

¾ of 600 = 0.75 x 600 = **450 really strange people**

2

To everything, tern, tern, tern ...

11,000 miles one way = 22,000 miles per year

22,000 x 20 years = **440,000 frequent flier miles**

3

Skin droppings

10 billion over 24 hours

$\frac{1}{24}$ x 10 billion over 1 hour

10 billion ÷ 24 = 0.4166666 billion over 1 hour

20 minutes = ⅓ of one hour

⅓ x 0.41666666 billion =

0.41666666 billion ÷ 3 = 0.1388888 billion skin scales

or 0.1388888 billion x 1,000 = 138.88 million skin scales

or **138,880,000 skin scales**

(Don't you wish you used Denorex™?)

4 Lumps in the gravy

48 ounces - 26 ounces which went through = 22 ounces did not

22/48 = 22 ÷ 48 = .458333 = 45.8% (46%) questionable lumps

5 Gum on the seats

2 out of 3 = ⅔ have gum

2/3 of 57,600 = ⅔ x 57,600 =

Because it says "exactly" we need to use precisely ⅔, not 0.666 or any other rounding.

⅓ of 57,600 = 57,600 ÷ 3 = 19,200

⅔ of 57,600 = 19,200 x 2 = **38,400 gum-stuck seats**

What flavors? **If you actually tried to figure out what flavors, you must have way too much free time.**

6 School bell

4.5 centimeters x 118 decibels = **531 centimeters or 5.31 meters**

(What'd you say? Speak up.)

7 Taj Mahal

cubic feet = length x width x depth

110 x 25 x 2 = **5,500 cubic-foot bricks**

Longest toe

OF STUDENTS

18	
15	
12	
9	
6	
3	

big toe   second toe   middle toe   second-to-last toe   pinky toe

8

Lawn ornaments

9

20,000 people ÷ 5 people per house = 4,000 houses

☞   18%   Snow White and the seven dwarfs
0.18 x 4,000 = 720 houses

☞   7% crystal balls
0.07 x 4,000 = 280 houses

☞   6%   Mexican boys
0.06 x 4,000 = 240 houses

☞   14% squirrels and bunnies
0.14 x 4,000 = 560 houses

☞   17% Bambi and her relatives
0.17 x 4,000 = 680 houses

☞   25% black boys fishing
0.25 x 4,000 = 1000 houses

☞   3% white boys fishing
0.03 x 4,000 = 120 houses

10 Beetle in the soup

$${}^{300,000}\!/_{12,000,000} = {}^{300}\!/_{12,000} = {}^{3}\!/_{120} = \mathbf{1/40}$$

¼₀ = 1 ÷ 40 = 0.025 = **2.5%** (including cockroach, ladybug, and Volkswagen)

11 School janitor

a)   Total = **2,566 artifacts**

b)   How many more chawed off pencils did she find than wads of gum?

Wads of gum = 17 + 18 + 11 = 46

2,184 chawed off pencils - 46 = **2138 more**

c)   What is the ratio of detention slips to permission slips?

12 detention to 14 permission = ¹²⁄₁₄ = ⁶⁄₇ or **6 to 7** or **6:7**

d)   What percent of the total garbage was the arthropod?

½₅₆₆ = 1 ÷ 2566 = 0.0003897

To find percent, multiply the decimal by 100.

0.0003897 x 100 = **0.03897%**

12 Acres of pizza

32,850 acres a year ÷ 365 days in a year **= 90 acres of pizza/day**

(Would you like that delivered, or do you plan to eat it here?)

Cans of Spam™

40 tons x 2,000 pounds per ton = 80,000 pounds of Spam™

80,000 pounds x 4 cans/pound = **320,000 cans of Spam™**

Pair of socks

2 x 365 = 730 days straight wearing

730 x 190 mg = **138,700 mg heavier** or **138.7 grams heavier**

(Every 6-8 weeks, he empties them out.)

Birthday cake

Not far. It died. But had it survived, it would have travelled

9" + 13" + 9" + 13" = **44"**

Staring mites

8.5 inches x 11 inches = 93.5 square inches

93.5 x 5 million = There mite be **467.5 million** or **467,500,000 mites**

Chicken noodle sloop

800 x ⅔ = 533⅓ = **533 large colonies of bacteria**

18 Candy jar

⅔ of 12 = ⅔ x 12 = **8 deadly butterscotch candies**

19 Frog eggs

We bet you thought:

147 x 3,000 = 441,000 eggs will hatch + 147 males + 147 females

Well, you're wrong! Frog eggs hatch into tadpoles, duh!

The only frogs surrounding you are the same ones that were there when you got in —

147 males + 147 females = **394 frogs**

20 Eyelash mites

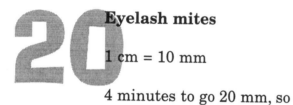

1 cm = 10 mm

4 minutes to go 20 mm, so

2 minutes to go 10 mm

21 Old, fuzzy grapes

David has eaten ⅔ of 62 = ⅔ x 62 = 41⅓ grapes

14% of 41⅓ grapes = 5.7866662 = **5 or 6 grapes**

(He's still chewing the sixth moldy, fuzzy grape.)

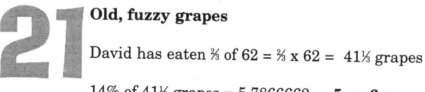

Interruptions

320 ideas x .75 = 240 ideas interrupted

⅓ x 240 = 80 return later

240 lost - 80 which return = **160 ideas lost per day**, and the world is a better place as a result

Blood vessel stretch

62,000 miles of blood vessels ÷ 2,451 miles = 25.295797 trips

NY to LA = 1 trip

LA to NY = 2 trips

So, the odd numbered trips end in LA, and the even numbered trips end in NY.

Therefore, 25.29 trips would **end closer to LA**. (unless you get lost and end up in Marshfield, Wisconsin, in which case be sure to look us up — or down)

Brain megabytes

100 trillion bits ÷ 8 = 12.5 trillion bytes

12.5 trillion bytes ÷ 1,024 = 0.012207 trillion kilobytes

0.012207 trillion = 12.207 billion

12.207 billion kilobytes ÷ 1,024 = 0.0119208 billion megabytes

0.0119208 billion = **close to 12 million megabytes**

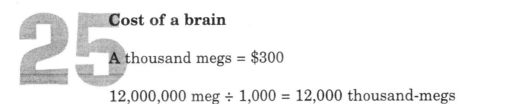

25 Cost of a brain

A thousand megs = $300

12,000,000 meg ÷ 1,000 = 12,000 thousand-megs

12,000 x $300 = **about $3,600,000.00**   (slightly more in Canada)

26 Make up your own problem

Example: How many times faster does the computer run?

120 ÷ 25 = 4.8 times faster

27 David's bandage

32,000,000 x 10,000 = 320,000,000,000 = **320 billion bacteria** in happy coexistence

28 Frequent indigestion

17 out of 1,000 = $^{17}/_{1,000}$ = 1.7/100 = 1.7%, so:

☞   Only eat pizza
1.7% x 364 = 0.017 x 364 = **6.188**
(or 6, and 1 with a queasy feeling)

☞   Sub in less than 65 seconds
0.017 x 325 = **5.525**

☞   25% in less than 10 seconds
0.25 x 5.525 = **1.38**

☞   Monosodium glutomate
0.017 x 274 = **4.658**

☞   Won't go to waste
0.017 x 472 = **8.024**

☞ Coupon people
  0.017 x 625 = **10.625**

☞ Peas porridge
  0.017 x 170 = **2.89**

☞ Gravy eaters
  0.017 x 69 = **1.173**

☞ Jellyfish sandwiches
  0.017 x 12 = **0.204**

Bats in the tent

27,000 mosquitoes ÷3,000 per bat = **9 bats needed** (or one superbat)

29

Cereal boxes

Wheat bran flakes 12 months ÷ 4 months = 3 boxes - the one they have

30

Frosted Mini-Wheats™   52 weeks ÷ 3.5 weeks = 14.85 boxes = 15 boxes - the one the have

Rice Krispies™   52 weeks ÷ 4 weeks = 13 boxes - the one they have

Cheerios™   52 ÷ 1.5 weeks = 34.6666= 35 boxes - the one they have

Apple Squares   52 ÷ 1 week = 52 boxes - the one they have

All Bran   0

2 + 14 + 12 + 34 + 51 + 0 = She will buy **113 boxes of cereal**

However, you may disagree with us. You may disagree with each other. In that case, how about a debate … or a duel?

31 Lucky Charms™

March 28 through the 31st = 4 days
(count it on your fingers if you don't believe us.)

April	30 days
May	31 days
June	30 days
July	31 days
August	31 days
September	30 days

Total 187 days of putting little yellow moon marshmallows in his closet

187 days x 17 little yellow moon marshmallows = **3,179 marshmallows**

32 Back yard fertilizer

100' x 100' = 10,000 square feet total

You walk on 10 sq ft out of 10,000 sq ft = $\frac{1}{1,000}$ of lawn's area

If you walked on the whole yard, you would step on 400 droppings.

Walking on $\frac{1}{1,000}$ of the yard, your odds are $\frac{1}{1,000}$ x 400 = $\frac{40}{100}$ or **4 out of 10** or **40%**

Unfortunately, you beat the odds.

33 Grocery store bulletin board

Hey man, you want us to do all the work?

Watch beeps

⅞ of 32 = ⅞ x 32 = **28 students** will be detained for questioning

34

Bacteria lifespan

20 minutes. Anybody who had anything else can go sit in the hall.

35

Leeches

90 pounds x 8 = 720 pounds of pop

16 ounces in a pound

720 x 16 = 11,520 ounces

11520 ounces ÷ 12 ounces in a can = **960 cans of pop**

And now for extra added torture, how many 24-can cases would that be?

36

Bath

50,000 on your back x 3 = **150,000 bacteria**

200,000 on your forehead x 3 = **600,000 bacteria**

1,000,000 in your armpit x 3 = **3,000,000 bacteria**

1,500,000 on your scalp x 3 = **4,500,000 bacteria**

(Asa and David have sworn off baths for the duration of their lives)

38 Crocodiles

2,000 people out of 5.9 billion people

$5,900,000,000 \div 2,000 = 2,950,000$

Your chances of being eaten are **1 in 2,950,000**

(except for the fact that there is one lurking under your bed at this very moment)

39 Cow gas

300,000 tons per day x 2,000 pounds in a ton = 600,000,000 pounds

$1.25 a pound x 600,000,000 pounds = **$750,000,000.00**

40 Skunk spray

It is very useful if you draw a diagram, and you're out of luck if you don't know $A = \pi r^2$.

area = 3.14 x (1 x 1)

area = **3.14 square miles**

41 Sneeze

A sneeze travels 104 miles in 1 hour = 60 minutes

There are 60 seconds in 1 minute.

60 minutes/hr x 60 seconds/min = 3,600 seconds/hr

2.5 seconds is what part of an hour?

2.5 ÷3600 = 0.0006944 of an hour

Remember, this decimal is part of a whole, and whenever we want to find part of something, we multiply.

Sneeze travels 104 miles in 1 hour

0.0006944 hr x 104 miles/hr = 0.0722176 mi

5,280 feet/mi x 0.0722176 mi= **381.3 feet**

Taste buds

9,000 taste buds x 47% burned off

9,000 x 0.47 = 4,230 burned off

9,000 - 4230 = **4,770 taste buds left**

Tick eating habits

7 years to ⅕ day

365 days x 7 = 2,555 (plus 1 or 2 leap days) = 2,556 or 2,557 days

2,556 or 2,557 days to ⅕ days

⅕ x 5 = 1

2,556 x 5 = 12,780

2557 x 5 = 12785

Americans eat 12,780 or 12,785 times more often than ticks.

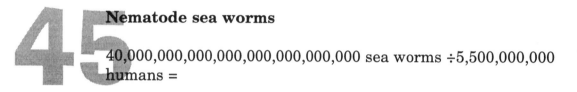

44 Overflow

1.5 gallons per flush

City can handle 3 x 100,000 gallons = 300,000 gallons

300,000 gallons ÷ 1.5 gallons/flush = **200,000 toilets flushing**

(Synchronize watch for 6:35 p.m. tonight.)

45 Nematode sea worms

40,000,000,000,000,000,000,000,000 sea worms ÷5,500,000,000 humans =

Cancel out the zeros.

400 quadrillion sea worms ÷ 55 humans = 7.27272727272 quadrillion

7,272,727,272,727,272 sea worms per person

Have you ever noticed how people resemble their pets?

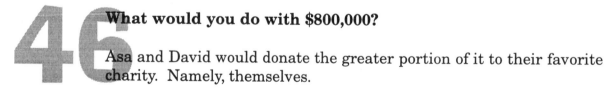

46 What would you do with $800,000?

Asa and David would donate the greater portion of it to their favorite charity. Namely, themselves.

47 Pumping Lake Michigan dry

1,300,000,000,000,000 gallons ÷ 2,000 gallons per day =

1,300,000,000,000 gallons ÷ 2 = 650,000,000,000 days

650 billion days ÷ 365.25 days/yr = 1.779603 billion years

It would take **1,779,603,000 years**.

You may begin.

Worms on the football field

Aha, we tricked you. This problem could be worked out by finding out the area of a football field, then dividing the area (square yards) by 4,840 square yards to find what part of an acre is a football field, then finding 1/10th of that, and then multiplying by 3 worms per acre. Too bad though, we can't do it. In order to find the area of the football field, we have to multiply length times width. We know the length (100 yards), but what's the width?

So the answer is "**not enough information**." The rest of you suckers wasted a lot of time.

*(EDITOR'S NOTE: It is possible that a few football fanatics were aware that the width of a football field is 55 yards. The answer could then be calculated at **340,909.1 worms**. Now the question is what is .1 worm?)*

Did you remember to flush?

$23.4 million dollars ÷ 1,209 times used = $ 0.0193548 million/flush

$ 0.0193548 million/flush x 1,000,000 =

Move the decimal point six places to the right.

It cost **$19,354.83 per flush**

Giant squid eyeball

volume of sphere = ⅓ x π x r³

radius = ½ diameter = 15 ÷ 2 = 7.5 inches

vol = ⅓ x 3.14 x (7.5 x 7.5 x 7.5)

vol = 1.33 x 3.14 x (7.5 x 7.5 x 7.5)

vol = 1.33 x 3.14 x 421.875

vol = **1,761.83 cubic inches of eyeball juice**

How many didn't bite?

25 million assorted insects over every square mile

10 sq mi x 25 million insects = 250 million insects over Camp Torture

Asa was bitten by 1,738 insects.

250,000,000 - 1,738 = **249,998,262 insects did not bite Asa**

Mirror, mirror, on the wall

14% of (24 hours/day - 8 hours sleeping)

0.14 x (24-8) = 0.14 x 16 = **2.24 hours per day**

Or to be more specific:

0.24 x 60 = 14.40 = **2 hours 14 minutes 24 seconds**

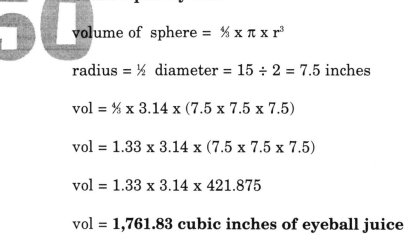

Special Thanks

We owe anywhere from begrudging thanks to undying gratitude
to the following people. We'll let them figure out which.

Dana
Taco Bell
Mom, Dad
Hormel Foods
Monty Python
Prufrock Press
Blue Bunny Popsicles
the guy in the trench coat
whomever bought this book
Grandma and Grandpa Ford
Scotty Shaw, proofreader, 5th grade
Carrie, Carmen, and Esther Washington
Marshfield Public Library Research Librarian

About the Authors

Asa and David are two computer geeks who are hopeless misfits and have no lives whatsoever. After doing this book, you will come to see why.

Asa Kleiman has gone completely insane, but hides it relatively well.

David Washington is normal in comparison, which doesn't count for much. He admits he can be extremely annoying, but he denies the frog incident entirely.

Denial

Mary feels bad that this book is not always nice to girls, but it is also not always nice to boys, and Asa and David say if you want to write a math book that's nicer to girls, go ahead.